LEWIS BROWN

DISASTROUS PART OF HURRICANE IAN

DANGER AND HAZARDOUS OUTCOMES OF HURRICANE IAN IN FLORIDA

Table of content

Chapter 3- Extreme danger in Florida

Introduction

<u>Keywords</u>

1. *disastrous hurricanes*

2. *disastrous part of hurricane ian and sylvia*

3. *disastrous part of hurricane ian astbury*

4. *disastrous part of hurricane ian desmond*

5. *disastrous part of hurricane ian east*

6. *disastrous part of hurricane ian eastwood*

<u>Book description</u>

The tempest is conveying a devastating trifecta of high breezes, weighty downpour and noteworthy tempest flood to the state and is set to cause critical blackouts and flooding as it moves at a sluggish speed across focal Florida over the course of the following little while.

Typhoon Ian is tied for the most grounded tempest to make landfall on the west shoreline of the Florida promontory, matching the breeze speed of Tropical storm Charley in 2004.

Chapter 1

Typhoon Ian to Make Landfall in Florida as 'Devastating' Tempest

Typhoon Ian is conjecture to make landfall in southwestern Florida in the following couple of hours as a "devastating" storm that is on the "limit of Classification 5 status," as per the

Public Tropical storm Community.

Storm floods of 12-18 feet over the ground level are normal along the southwest Florida shoreline from Englewood to Bonita Ocean side, the middle wrote in its

Wednesday update.

"Occupants here ought to desperately follow any departure orders in actuality," the middle composed.

Chapter 2

Change in Hurricane Ian could cause 30 billion dollar catastrophe for Florida

A change in Hurricane Ian could see a 30 billion dollar catastrophe come to individuals of Florida in the event that it causes a landfall.

The normal track of the tempest has changed marginally and that could influence the populace focal point of Tampa and the inadequately populated beg region of the state next Thursday.

Ian's top breezes arrived at 45 miles each hour, around 300 miles south-southeast of Kingston, Jamaica early Saturday, as indicated by the US Public Tropical storm Community.

Typhoon Ian is ready to become one of the costliest tempests in U.S. history, leaving a horrendous path of floods and power disappointments in

Cuba and taking steps to hammer Florida's western shoreline next with 125-mile-per-hour winds.

Ian's top breezes have dropped to 115 mph as it

reappeared over the southeastern Inlet of Mexico, around 305 miles (491 kilometers) from Sarasota, Florida, as indicated by a warning from the US Public Tropical storm Community at 11 a.m. New York time.

The tempest is conjecture to reinforce through Wednesday, bringing dangers of 8-foot storm floods into Tampa Straight and weighty downpours across the US Southeast.

Harms and monetary misfortunes in the space could reach $45 billion to $70 billion if the ebb and flow gauge happens . The top finish of that reach would rank Ian as the 6th costliest U.S. storm, as indicated by information from the Public Maritime and Barometrical

Organization. The tempest comes as environmental change fills outrageous climate around the world, including storms that quickly gain strength as they approach land. The year has proactively gotten destructive flooding Kentucky, an European intensity wave that killed in excess of 2,000 individuals in Portugal and Spain, and more steady dry spell holding the Western US and a significant storm that passed on

disastrous harm
from Puerto Rico
to Atlantic Canada
— every fiasco
demanding its
own human and
monetary cost.

Chapter 3

EXTREME DANGER IN FLORIDA

Forecasters say Typhoon Ian is supposed to cause perilous tempest floods, horrendous breezes and flooding in the Florida landmass, as well as impressive glimmer, metropolitan and stream flooding as it crosses focal Florida Wednesday night and Thursday prior to reappearing over the western Atlantic Sea. Ian is additionally expected to create however much 60 centimeters of downpour from the Florida Keys and South Florida into the adjoining provinces of Georgia and South Carolina.

Streak floods were conceivable the whole way across Florida, with the tempest expected to pound the Orlando region Thursday and leave the state close to Daytona Ocean side. Government authorities said

Tuesday that inland flooding was their greatest wellbeing concerns.